AUTHENTIC / TRADITIONAL PIEROGI RECIPES

Discover The Simple Art of Making Pierogi at Home with A Wide Variety of Main and Desert Pierogi Recipes to Suit Every Taste.

ANNA NOVAK

INTRODUCTION

Pierogi have been shared over the dinner table in Poland and other Slavic countries since the Middle Ages. In fact, it has been a part of the staple diet since this time. Back in those times Pierogi were only consumed by farmers and the poor, until one day someone of higher status tried one and fell in love at first bite!

Today we are thankful because so many centuries of trial and error in Pierogi recipes have passed. Today Pierogi are loved all over the world!

Now I want to share a wide variety of recipes with you, some dating back to the Middle Ages. There are many modern twists and variations to Pierogi, however my aim is to provide you with traditional and authentic recipes. Each and every recipe is easy to follow and can be simply recreated at home.

All recipes in this book were given the tick of approval from my 89-year-old grandmother (Babcia.)

TABLE OF CONTENTS

DEDICATION

This book is dedicated to my beautiful children, Hania and Milosz. They have taught me so many life lessons and so much about myself. I love you with all my heart.

MAKING THE DOUGH

THE SIMPLEST AND FASTEST WAY!

There are many recipes for pierogi dough, some include milk, some exclude eggs, some are traditional and some are not. Below are the ingredients and preparation method for the most traditional method of making the Pierogi dough.

INGREDIENTS:

- 2,5 cups of plain flour (500g)
- 1 whole egg
- 1 cup of lukewarm water
- 3 tablespoons olive oil
- Pinch of salt

PREPARATION:

1. Add 2 cups flour in a large bowl or work surface and make a well in the center. Break the egg into it, add the salt, olive oil and a little lukewarm water

at a time. Bring the dough together, kneading well while adding more flour or water if necessary. Put dough into a bowl, cover with cloth or plate and allow to rest 20 minutes.

2. On a floured work surface, roll the dough out thinly and cut with a 2-inch round cutter or glass.

Please note* Rather than adding the dough making instructions to each of the recipes below, please refer back to this section.

CHAPTER 1: MAIN DISH PIEROGI
PIEROGI RUSKIE

INGREDIENTS FOR THE FILLING:

- 4 big potatoes
- 1 tablespoon butter
- 150g of ricotta cheese (Or white polish cheese)
- Salt, pepper
- 1 onion
- A couple of leaves of fresh mint
- Marjoram, oregano
- Bacon

* Prepare The dough 20 minutes prior to starting on filling. FOR THE DOUGH INSTRUCTIONS PLEASE REFER TO 'MAKING DOUGH SECTION" ON PAGE 6 *

PREPARATION FOR THE FILLING:

1. Peel and dice potatoes. Add to boiling water and allow to boil for 20 mins. Add a pinch of salt. When

cooked and softened, drain water then add cheese and mix until mixture has a smooth consistency.

TIP: The best pierogi are made from fresh, flexible filling.

2. Sauté finely chopped onion on melted butter and add salt, marjoram, oregano. Add this to the pot with our potato and cheese mix. Mix all together. (for best mixing results, the potatoes and cheese should still be warm.)

3. Using a tablespoon, spoon filling into dough. Fold over and pinch to close, making sure the pierogi are sealed.

4. Sprinkle a baking tray with flour and place the filled pierogi on it and cover with tea towel. Bring a large saucepan of salted water to boil. Drop in the pierogi (around 8 per time.) When the pierogi rise to the surface, simmer for 2 more minutes.

5. Remove pierogis and allow to drain.

Traditionally "Ruskie Pierogi" are served with fried off bacon cubes. This only takes a few minutes so I usually do this while the pierogis are draining.

6. Once pierogis are drained and bacon is fried, serve hot and enjoy.

PIEROGI WITH MINCED MEAT

INGREDIENTS FOR THE FILLING:

- 1 kg minced meat (beef, chicken or turkey)
- Salt, pepper
- 1 onion
- 1/2 cup stock (use appropriate stock for your selected minced meat)

* Prepare The dough 20 minutes prior to starting on filling. FOR THE DOUGH INSTRUCTIONS PLEASE REFER TO 'MAKING DOUGH SECTION" ON PAGE 6 *

PREPARATION FOR THE FILLING:

1. Chop and dice onion. Over med-high heat in a large saucepan add a tablespoon of oil and sauté onion for around 2 minutes or until cooked. Add minced meat and combine with the onion. Fry on high heat until meat is browned, reduce the heat to medium and add stock, pinch of salt and pepper and allow to cook through, around 10 minutes or until all is cooked and the stock is reduced.

2. Remove off heat and let cool slightly before adding the filling to your pre prepared pierogi dough. (Depending on how "chunky" you like the filling, you may also like to use a potato masher to make the consistency of the filling smoother.)

3. Using a tablespoon, spoon filling into dough. Fold over and pinch to close, making sure the pierogis are sealed.

4. Sprinkle a baking tray with flour and place the filled pierogi on it and cover with tea towel. Bring a large saucepan of salted water to boil. Drop in the pierogi (around 8 per time.) When the pierogi rise to the surface, simmer for 2 more minutes.

5. Remove pierogis and allow to drain.

*Traditionally "Pierogi with meat" are served with fried onion pieces. This only takes a minute so I usually do this while the pierogis are draining.

6. Once pierogis are drained and onion is fried, serve hot and enjoy.

PIEROGI WITH BUCKWHEAT GROATS

INGREDIENTS FOR THE FILLING:

- 2 glasses of buckwheat groats
- Salt, pepper
- 1 onion
- 100g Bacon
- Olive oil

* Prepare The dough 20 minutes prior to starting on filling. FOR THE DOUGH INSTRUCTIONS PLEASE REFER TO 'MAKING DOUGH SECTION" ON PAGE 6 *

PREPARATION FOR THE FILLING:

1. Cook buckwheat groats in large pot of salted water, usually 10-15 minutes

2. While groats are cooking, finely chop and dice onion and sauté for 2 minutes or until cooked. Dice bacon and fry in same pan for a further 2 minutes or until bacon is cooked.

3. Once buckwheat groats are cooked, drain and return to the same large pot, add a pinch or salt and pepper, add bacon and onion and mix all together, until well combined.

4. Using a tablespoon, spoon filling into dough. Fold over and pinch to close, making sure the pierogis are sealed.

5. Sprinkle a baking tray with flour and place the filled pierogi on it and cover with tea towel. Bring a large saucepan of salted water to boil. Drop in the pierogi (around 8 per time.) When the pierogi rise to the surface, simmer for 2 more minutes.

6. Remove pierogis and allow to drain.

7. Melt butter and pour it on the pierogi before serving

PIEROGI WITH POTATOES AND PEAS

INGREDIENTS FOR THE FILLING:

- 4 big potatoes
- Salt, pepper
- 1 onion
- 200g of frozen pees
- Olive oil

* Prepare The dough 20 minutes prior to starting on filling. FOR THE DOUGH INSTRUCTIONS PLEASE REFER TO 'MAKING DOUGH SECTION" ON PAGE 6 *

PREPARATION FOR THE FILLING:

1. Peel and dice potatoes. Add to boiling water and allow to boil for 20 mins. Add a pinch of salt. When cooked and softened, drain water.

2. Using a different pot, Add the peas to boiling water and allow to boil for 10-15 minutes, or until soft. Drain water.

3. While potatoes and peas are still hot add them to one pot and mash together, add a pinch of salt and pepper.

4. Using a tablespoon, spoon filling into dough. Fold over and pinch to close, making sure the pierogis are sealed.

5. Sprinkle a baking tray with flour and place the filled pierogi on it and cover with tea towel. Bring a large saucepan of salted water to boil. Drop in the pierogi (around 8 per time.) When the pierogi rise to the surface, simmer for 2 more minutes.

6. Remove pierogis and allow to drain.

7. Melt butter and pour it on the pierogi before serving

PIEROGI WITH MUSHROOMS AND ONION

INGREDIENTS FOR THE FILLING:

- 500g of mushrooms (forest mushrooms are best, but any mushrooms are fine)
- Salt, pepper
- 2 ½ onions
- 1 tablespoon of butter
- *Bread crumbs (if needed)*

* Prepare The dough 20 minutes prior to starting on filling. FOR THE DOUGH INSTRUCTIONS PLEASE REFER TO 'MAKING DOUGH SECTION" ON PAGE 6 *

PREPARATION FOR THE FILLING:

1. Chop and dice mushrooms and onions. Add butter to hot fry pan. Add salt and pepper and Sauté mushrooms and onions for 2 minutes or until cooked. (be very careful not to let this mixture become watery, if this happens add bread crumbs

to the mix to reduce and remove water.) when satisfied, remove off heat.

2. Using a tablespoon, spoon filling into dough. Fold over and pinch to close, making sure the pierogis are sealed.

3. Sprinkle a baking tray with flour and place the filled pierogi on it and cover with tea towel. Bring a large saucepan of salted water to boil. Drop in the pierogi (around 8 per time.) When the pierogi rise to the surface, simmer for 2 more minutes.

4. Remove pierogis and allow to drain.

5. Melt butter and pour it on the pierogi before serving

PIEROGI WITH MUSHROOMS AND SAUERKRAUT

INGREDIENTS FOR THE FILLING:

- *500g of mushrooms (forest mushrooms are best, but any mushrooms are fine)
- 1kg of sauerkraut
- 1 ½ onion
- Butter

* Prepare The dough 20 minutes prior to starting on filling. FOR THE DOUGH INSTRUCTIONS PLEASE REFER TO 'MAKING DOUGH SECTION" ON PAGE 6 *

PREPARATION FOR THE FILLING:

1. Finely chop and dice onion and sauté for 2 minutes or until cooked.

2. Remove all juice from sauerkraut and add drained sauerkraut to sautéed onion. Add salt and pepper and allow to cook for 5 minutes.

3. Using a tablespoon, spoon filling into dough. Fold over and pinch to close, making sure the pierogis are sealed.

4. Sprinkle a baking tray with flour and place the filled pierogi on it and cover with tea towel. Bring a large saucepan of salted water to boil. Drop in the pierogi (around 8 per time.) When the pierogi rise to the surface, simmer for 2 more minutes.

5. Remove pierogis and allow to drain.

*Traditionally "Pierogi with mushrooms and sauerkraut" are served with fried onion pieces and melted butter. This only takes a minute so I usually do this while the pierogis are draining.

6. Once pierogis are drained, onion is fried and butter is melted, drizzle over pierogis before serving.

PIEROGI WITH FETA CHEESE AND OLIVES

INGREDIENTS FOR THE FILLING:

- 500g of feta cheese
- 200g of black olives (sliced)
- Butter

* Prepare The dough 20 minutes prior to starting on filling. FOR THE DOUGH INSTRUCTIONS PLEASE REFER TO 'MAKING DOUGH SECTION" ON PAGE 6 *

PREPARATION FOR THE FILLING:

1. Mix feta cheese with olives in a large bowl. There is no need to add anything extra as feta and olives have strong taste.

2. Using a tablespoon, spoon filling into dough. Fold over and pinch to close, making sure the pierogis are sealed.

3. Sprinkle a baking tray with flour and place the filled pierogi on it and cover with tea towel. Bring a large saucepan of salted water to boil. Drop in the pierogi (around 8 per time.) When the pierogi rise to the surface, simmer for 2 more minutes.

4. Remove pierogis and allow to drain.

5. Melt butter and pour it on the pierogi before serving

PIEROGI WITH SPINACH AND RICOTTA CHEESE

INGREDIENTS FOR THE FILLING:

- 400 g of spinach (may be even frozen)
- 400 g ricotta cheese
- 2 big onions
- 4 garlic cloves
- Salt, pepper
- Butter

* Prepare The dough 20 minutes prior to starting on filling. FOR THE DOUGH INSTRUCTIONS PLEASE REFER TO 'MAKING DOUGH SECTION" ON PAGE 6 *

PREPARATION FOR THE FILLING:

1. Chop and dice onions. Mince garlic and sauté for 2 minutes in deep saucepan.

2. Add ricotta cheese to saucepan with the onion and garlic and fork blend until combined (the reason

for fork blending is because it adds a layer of texture.)

3. Using a tablespoon, spoon filling into dough. Fold over and pinch to close, making sure the pierogis are sealed.

4. Sprinkle a baking tray with flour and place the filled pierogi on it and cover with tea towel. Bring a large saucepan of salted water to boil. Drop in the pierogi (around 8 per time.) When the pierogi rise to the surface, simmer for 2 more minutes.

5. Remove pierogis and allow to drain.

6. Melt butter and pour it on the pierogi before serving

CHAPTER 2: SWEET PIEROGI
PIEROGI WITH CREAM CHEESE

INGREDIENTS FOR THE FILLING:

- 1 egg yoke
- 500 g cream cheese
- 1 tablespoon Vanilla extract
- 4 teaspoons of sugar
- *Cinamon, raisins (optional)*
- *Cream (optional)*

* Prepare The dough 20 minutes prior to starting on filling. FOR THE DOUGH INSTRUCTIONS PLEASE REFER TO 'MAKING DOUGH SECTION" ON PAGE 6 *

PREPARATION OF THE FILLING:

1. In a large mixing bowl add cream cheese, vanilla extract and sugar, mix until well combined, around 1 minute

2. Using a tablespoon, spoon filling into dough. Fold over and pinch to close, making sure the pierogis are sealed.

3. Sprinkle a baking tray with flour and place the filled pierogi on it and cover with tea towel. Bring a large saucepan of salted water to boil. Drop in the pierogi (around 8 per time.) When the pierogi rise to the surface, simmer for 2 more minutes.

4. Remove pierogis and allow to drain.

5. Traditionally these pierogis are served with a topping of cream, cinnamon and raisins. To make this topping simply combine all ingredients in a mixing bowl (making sure that it's not too thick.)

6. Serve hot

PIEROGI WITH BLACKBERRIES (AND CREAM CHEESE).

Pierogi's may be made with cheese or without it.

INGREDIENTS FOR THE DOUGH:

- 500g of flour
- ½ liter of buttermilk

PREPARATION OF THE DOUGH:

1. Mix the ingredients together until it is smooth and ready to roll on the pastry board. If it is too dry add more buttermilk and if it is too watery add more flour.

2. Divide it into smaller pieces and roll, ensuring that the dough does not stuck to the pastry board.

INGREDIENTS OF THE FILLING:

- 300g of blackberries
- 250g of cream cheese
- 2 teaspoons of sugar
- *Cream (optional)*

PREPARATION OF THE FILLING:

1. Mix blackberries, sugar and cream cheese (if you chose the version with cream cheese). Taste it to check if it is sweet enough. Put more sugar if needed.

2. Using a tablespoon, spoon filling into dough. Fold over and pinch to close, making sure the pierogis are sealed.

3. Sprinkle a baking tray with flour and place the filled pierogi on it and cover with tea towel. Bring a large saucepan of salted water to boil. Drop in the pierogi (around 8 per time.) When the pierogi rise to the surface, simmer for 2 more minutes.

4. Remove pierogis and allow to drain.

5. Traditionally these pierogis are served with a topping of cream and sugar. To make this topping simply combine all ingredients in a mixing bowl (making sure that it's not too thick.)

PIEROGI WITH STRAWBERRIES (OR ANY OTHER SEASONAL FRUIT E.G. PLUMS, CHERRIES, PEACHES)

INGREDIENTS FOR THE FILLING:

- 200g of strawberries or other fruit
- Sugar
- *Cream (optional)*

* Prepare The dough 20 minutes prior to starting on filling. FOR THE DOUGH INSTRUCTIONS PLEASE REFER TO 'MAKING DOUGH SECTION" ON PAGE 6 *

PREPARATION OF THE FILLING:

1. Cut Strawberries or chosen fruit into smaller pieces so that it will be easy to fork blend. Add cut fruit and sugar to mixing bowl and mix until you are happy with its consistency.

2. Using a tablespoon, spoon filling into dough. Fold over and pinch to close, making sure the pierogis are sealed.

3. Sprinkle a baking tray with flour and place the filled pierogi on it and cover with tea towel. Bring a large saucepan of salted water to boil. Drop in the pierogi (around 8 per time.) When the pierogi rise to the surface, simmer for 2 more minutes.

4. Remove pierogis and allow to drain.

5. Traditionally these pierogis are served with a topping of cream and sugar. To make this topping simply combine all ingredients in a mixing bowl (making sure that it's not too thick.)

CHOCOLATE PIEROGI WITH RASPBERRIES, MINT AND WHITE CHOCOLATE

INGREDIENTS FOR THE DOUGH:

- 500g of flour
- 2 teaspoons of real cocoa
- 1 whole egg
- 1 egg yoke
- Pinch of salt
- Hot water

*Please follow the "making dough instructions" on page 6. The only thing that has changed are the ingredients which are listed above. *

INGREDIENTS OF THE FILLING:

- 300g of raspberries
- 50g of white chocolate
- a few leaves of fresh mint
- *Vanilla ice cream (optional)*

PREPARATION OF THE FILLING:

1. Chop and crumble the white chocolate in a bowl, slice and add mint leaves. Add raspberries and combine the mixture. Don't worry if it appears to be a thick filling, the chocolate will melt while boiling, making it beautiful and smooth when cooked.

2. Using a tablespoon, spoon filling into dough. Fold over and pinch to close, making sure the pierogis are sealed.

3. Sprinkle a baking tray with flour and place the filled pierogi on it and cover with tea towel. Bring a large saucepan of salted water to boil. Drop in the pierogi (around 8 per time.) When the pierogi rise to the surface, simmer for 2 more minutes.

4. Remove pierogis and allow to drain.

5. Serve while hot and add ice-cream as a topping.

PIEROGI WITH APPLES AND CINNAMON

INGREDIENTS FOR THE FILLING:

- 3 apples
- Sugar
- Pinch of cinnamon
- Cream

* Prepare The dough 20 minutes prior to starting on filling. FOR THE DOUGH INSTRUCTIONS PLEASE REFER TO 'MAKING DOUGH SECTION" ON PAGE 6 *

PREPARATION OF THE FILLING:

1. Peel apples and cut them into small pieces, place in the pan and fry until they soft, add sugar and a pinch of cinnamon, cook for additional 2 minutes.

2. Using a tablespoon, spoon filling into dough. Fold over and pinch to close, making sure the pierogis are sealed.

3. Sprinkle a baking tray with flour and place the filled pierogi on it and cover with tea towel. Bring a large saucepan of salted water to boil. Drop in the pierogi (around 8 per time.) When the pierogi rise to the surface, simmer for 2 more minutes.

4. Remove pierogis and allow to drain. Serve hot.

PIEROGI WITH BANANAS AND DARK CHOCOLATE

INGREDIENTS FOR THE DOUGH:

- 3 glasses of flour
- ½ glass of semolina
- 1/3 glass of oil
- Pinch of salt
- 1 glass of hot water

* Prepare The dough 20 minutes prior to starting on filling. FOR THE DOUGH INSTRUCTIONS PLEASE REFER TO 'MAKING DOUGH SECTION" ON PAGE 6 *

INGREDIENTS FOR THE FILLING:

- 2-3 bananas
- Sugar
- 50g dark chocolate
- Cream

PREPARATION OF THE FILLING:

1. Mash bananas and add sugar, if bananas are sweet enough there is no need to put any sugar.

2. Cut and crumble dark chocolate, Add to the banana mix and combine well.

3. Using a tablespoon, spoon filling into dough. Fold over and pinch to close, making sure the pierogis are sealed.

4. Sprinkle a baking tray with flour and place the filled pierogi on it and cover with tea towel. Bring a large saucepan of salted water to boil. Drop in the pierogi (around 8 per time.) When the pierogi rise to the surface, simmer for 2 more minutes.

5. Remove pierogis and allow to drain. Serve hot and add cream as a sauce.

CHAPTER 3: UNIQUE DOUGH AND FILLINGS.

In this chapter I would like to show all other kinds of pierogi and all other kinds of doughs you can make pierogi from.

You can make all kinds of traditional filling, e.g. ruskie (with potatoes), mushroom and sauerkraut. Or you can choose one of my new recipes which you will find below.

But first see the recipes for different doughs:

YEAST DOUGH

INGREDIENTS:

- 20g of yeast
- 65 ml of milk
- 150g of butter
- 350g of flour
- 1 whole egg
- Pinch of salt and sugar

PREPARATION:

1. Before you start your work on the dough take the butter out of the fridge, it has to be in a room temperature.

2. Heat the milk. Sieve the flour on a pastry board and make a well, inside the well add salt, sugar, yeast and egg and cover everything with the heated milk.

3. Fill in well, scooping flour from the edges. Start kneading, and when the ingredients begin to combine, add the soft butter. Knead until the dough ceases to stick and will have dry, dull surface.

4. Put the kneaded dough in a bowl and leave in a warm place to rise until the dough will increase at least by half.

5. Now make the filling you choose. You can make all kinds of traditional filling, e.g. ruskie (with potatoes), mushroom and sauerkraut, you can choose my new recipes.

6. Preheat oven to 180 °. cover two large baking trays with sheets of baking paper. Hit the dough with the fist and insert it on the floured pastry board. Knead for a minute. Then roll out the dough

to a thickness of approx. 0.5 cm. Cut the small circles out and put on them on the 1/2 teaspoon of stuffing.

7. Form small pierogi and place them at baking tray in 3 centimeters in between the pierogi. When the sheet is full, paint dumplings with egg yolk and put into preheated oven.

8. Bake for 20-30 minutes, until pierogi are golden and shiny. During this time, knead scraps of dough, roll it out, cut circles and form next pierogi on the second tray. You should make approx. 25 pierogi.

SHORTCRUST DOUGH

INGREDIENTS:

- 200g of flour
- 120g of butter
- 2 egg yokes
- 1 spoon of sour cream
- Pinch of salt

PREPARATION:

1. Combine dough ingredients, chopping them first knife (butter should be soft) on the pastry board, then knead, form into a ball,

2. Wrap in plastic foil and leave for at least 30 minutes in the refrigerator. Remember that dough hates heat, so avoid touching it with your hands. Put it in the refrigerator as fast as possible.

3. Now is the time to make the chosen filling.

4. After at least 30 minutes roll the dough and cut the circles for the pierogi. Place filling in the middle and form pierogi. Brush the pierogi with the egg yolk and put in the oven heated to 180 °.

5. Bake for 20 minutes until they golden and shiny.

PUFF PASTRY

It is very difficult and time-consuming to make puff pastry from scratch that is why you may just buy premade pastry.

YEAST DOUGH PIEROGI WITH CHICKEN AND GARLIC SAUCE

* Prepare The dough 20 minutes prior to starting on filling. FOR THE DOUGH INSTRUCTIONS PLEASE REFER TO 'MAKING DOUGH SECTION" ON PAGE 6 *

INGREDIENTS FOR THE FILLING:

- 500g of chicken breast
- 2 pcs of red capsicums
- 300g of mushrooms
- 1 large onion
- 200g of cheddar cheese
- Chives, salt, pepper
- 1 Egg yolk

INGREDIENTS FOR THE SAUCE:

- 400g of Greek yoghurt
- 3 cloves of garlic
- Salt and pepper
- 1 table spoon of mustard
- Lemon juice

PREPARATION OF THE FILLING:

1. Cut chicken, capsicum and onions into small pieces,

2. Fry the chicken, add capsicums and salt and pepper to taste. Fry until chicken is browned, around 5 minutes.

3. Peel mushrooms and cut them into slices.

4. On a separate pan fry the mushrooms with onions. Mix all the ingredients, add the grated cheese and chopped chives.

5. Roll out the dough to a thickness of about 5mm, cut into large squares on the side of 10-12cm. At the center of each square place stuffing, forming pierogi. Cover the surface of pierogi with the yolk. Bake in 180° until they golden and shiny.

6. Prepare the sauce by mixing all ingredients. Put the sauce in the fridge to cool it down.

7. Serve the pierogi with the sauce on the side, sprinkled with chives.

YEAST PIEROGI WITH SPINACH AND GORGONZOLA CHEESE

* Prepare The dough 20 minutes prior to starting on filling. FOR THE DOUGH INSTRUCTIONS PLEASE REFER TO 'MAKING DOUGH SECTION" ON PAGE 6 *

INGREDIENTS FOR THE FILLING:

- Frozen or fresh spinach (one pack)
- 4 cloves of garlic
- 200g of gorgonzola cheese
- 2 tablespoons of sour cream
- Salt and pepper

PREPARATION OF THE FILLING:

1. Place spinach in a pot and cook it until thick and dry, around 3 minutes. *The less watery the easier it will be to put the stuffing in pierogi*. Add grated garlic cloves, crushed cheese, pepper and salt. Be careful because the cheese itself is salty. Add cream to make the filling nice and smooth.

2. Roll out the dough to a thickness of about 5mm, cut into large squares on the side of 10-12cm. At the center of each square place stuffing, forming pierogi. Cover the surface of pierogi with the yolk. Bake in 180° until they golden and shiny.

3. Optionally you can pour sour cream on the pierogi before serving.

SHORT CRUST PIEROGI WITH MEAT AND SESAME SEEDS

*Prepare The dough 20 minutes prior to starting on filling. FOR THE DOUGH INSTRUCTIONS PLEASE REFER TO 'MAKING DOUGH SECTION" ON PAGE 6 *

INGREDIENTS FOR THE FILLING:

- 250g of minced chicken or turkey meat
- 1 whole egg
- ½ big onion
- 1 tablespoon of flour
- Salt and pepper, basil, oregano
- 50g Sesame seeds

PREPARATION OF THE FILLING:

1. Chop and dice onion finely and fry in oil until cooked, around 2 minutes. Add meat of choice, egg, flour, salt and pepper to taste. Fry all ingredients until meat is cooked and mixture has become thick, around 10 minutes. Allow to cool down.

2. Preheat oven to 180

3. Place filling in the middle and form pierogi. Brush the pierogi with the egg yolk and sprinkle sesame seeds over and put in the oven heated to 180 °.

4. Bake for 20 minutes until they golden and shiny.

Short crust dessert pierogi with apples and white chocolate sauce

* Prepare The dough 20 minutes prior to starting on filling. FOR THE DOUGH INSTRUCTIONS PLEASE REFER TO 'MAKING DOUGH SECTION" ON PAGE 6 *

Ingredients for the filling:

- 500g of apples
- 50g of sugar
- 2 teaspoons of cinnamon
- 1 teaspoon of cardamom
- 1 tablespoon of corn flour
- 50g of white chocolate
- 2 table spoons of double cream

Preparation of the filling:

1. Peel the apples, grate half and the other half, chop finely. Mix the apples with sugar, cinnamon and cardamom. Add corn flour and mix everything. Put it away to the fridge for at least half an hour.

49

2. Roll the dough and cut the circles for the pierogi. Place filling in the middle and form pierogi. Cover the surface with the egg yolk Put in the oven heated to 180 °. Bake for 20 minutes until they golden and shiny.

3. Prepare the sauce. Pour warm cream on the white chocolate and mix it until chocolate melts. Pour the sauce over pierogi before serving.

PUFF PASTRY PIEROGI WITH MUSHROOMS (PERFECT TO GO WITH CLEAR BEETROOT SOUP)

- 500g of packet puff pastry – keep it in fridge till the filling is ready.

INGREDIENTS FOR THE FILLING:

- 500g of ground mushrooms
- 1 onion
- 1 clove of garlic
- Parsley
- Salt and pepper
- 1 whole egg

PREPARATION OF THE FILLING:

1. Chop the mushrooms and onion. Fry the onion and add mushrooms, salt and pepper to taste. When it is cooked, around 5 minutes, turn the heat off and add chopped parsley. Cool the filling down.

2. Rolll the dough and cut the circles for the pierogi. Place filling in the middle and form pierogi. Cover the surface with the egg yolk. Put in the oven heated to 200 °. Bake for 15 minutes until they golden and shiny.

PUFF PASTRY DESSERT'S PIEROGI WITH PEACHES

- 500g of packet puff pastry – keep it in fridge till the filling is ready.

INGREDIENTS FOR THE FILLING:

- 150 g of sugar
- 4 peaches
- 1 glass of semisweet white wine
- 2 tablespoons of flour

PREPARATION OF THE FILLING:

1. Peel the peaches. Boil in wine for 15 minutes or until it reduces by half, add sugar and cook for additional 5 minutes. Add flour and stir. Allow to cool

2. Roll the dough and cut the circles for the pierogi. Place filling in the middle and form pierogi. Cover the surface with the egg yolk and sesame seeds. Put in the oven heated to 200 °. Bake for 15 minutes until they golden and shiny.

Can I Ask a Favor?

If you enjoyed this book, found it useful or otherwise then I'd really appreciate it if you would post a short review on Amazon. I do read all the reviews personally so that I can continually write what people are wanting.

Thanks for your support!

Anna Novak

Printed in Great Britain
by Amazon